Sloths

By Laura Buller

Editors Sally Beets, Kritika Gupta
US Senior Editor Shannon Beatty
Designer Bettina Myklebust Stovne
Project Art Editor Rashika Kachroo
Assistant Art Editor Shubhi Srivastava
Jacket Coordinator Issy Walsh
Jacket Designer Dheeraj Arora
DTP Designers Dheeraj Singh, Vikram Singh
Picture Researcher Aditya Katyal
Producer, Pre-Production Dragana Puvacic
Producer Basia Ossowska
Managing Editors Laura Gilbert, Monica Saigal
Deputy Managing Art Editor Ivy Sengupta
Managing Art Editor Diane Peyton Jones
Delhi Team Head Malavika Talukder
Creative Director Helen Senior
Publishing Director Sarah Larter

Reading Consultant Linda Gambrell
Subject Consultant David Curnick

First American Edition, 2019
Published in the United States by DK Publishing
450 Broadway, Suite 801,
New York, NY 10018

The publisher would like to thank the following for their kind permission to reproduce their photographs:
(Key: a-above; b-below/bottom; c-center; f-far; l-left; r-right; t-top)

1 Alamy Stock Photo: robertharding / Marco Simoni. **3 Alamy Stock Photo**: Michael S. Nolan. **4 Alamy Stock Photo**: Oyvind Martinsen-Panama Wildlife. **5 Alamy Stock Photo**: Arco / G. Lacz. **6-7 Alamy Stock Photo**: Kevin Elsby. **8-9 Alamy Stock Photo**: FLPA. **10 Dreamstime.com**: Kungverylucky. **11 Depositphotos Inc**: kobbydagan. **12 Alamy Stock Photo**: Avalon / Photoshot License (br); National Geographic Image Collection / Cagan H. Sekercioglu (clb). **Dreamstime.com**: Wrangel (cl). **13 Dreamstime. com**: Kungverylucky (cl); Seadam (crb). **SuperStock**: Suzi Eszterhas / Minden Pictures (ca). **15 naturepl.com**: Suzi Eszterhas. **16-17 Alamy Stock Photo**: CarverMostardi. **18-19 Depositphotos Inc**: kengoru. **20-21 SuperStock**: Suzi Eszterhas / Minden Pictures. **23 Dreamstime.com**: Demerzel21 (cra); Inga Nielsen / Inganielsen (cla). **Getty Images**: Westend61 (crb). **SuperStock**: Suzi Eszterhas / Minden Pictures (clb). **24-25 Dreamstime.com**: Jorn Vangoidtsenhoven. **26 Depositphotos Inc**: photogallet. **27 Dreamstime.com**: Amilevin. **28-29 Alamy Stock Photo**: All Canada Photos / Barrett & MacKay. **30-31 FLPA**: Suzi Eszterhas / Minden Pictures (b). **31 Dorling Kindersley**: Wildlife Heritage Foundation, Kent, UK (cr). **Dreamstime.com**: Honourableandbold (cl). **32 Dreamstime.com**: Ignasi Such. **33 Alamy Stock Photo**: Kumar Sriskandan. **34-35 Getty Images**: © Juan Carlos Vindas. **36 Dreamstime.com**: Janossygergely. **37 Getty Images**: Moment Open / Seadance Photography. **39 Dreamstime.com**: Marco Díaz. **40 Dreamstime.com**: André Costa. **41 Alamy Stock Photo**: Rosanne Tackaberry (clb, crb). **42 Alamy Stock Photo**: The Natural History Museum (bl). **SuperStock**: Suzi Eszterhas / Minden Pictures (c). **43 Alamy Stock Photo**: Rosanne Tackaberry (c). **Depositphotos Inc**: janossygergely (cr). **Dreamstime.com**: Brian Magnier (ca)

Endpaper images: *Front and Back*: **Dreamstime.com**: Jonathan Ross

Cover images: *Front*: **Alamy Stock Photo**: Michael S. Nolan; *Back*: **Dreamstime.com**: Jenhuang99 (cla)

All other images © Dorling Kindersley
For further information see: www.dkimages.com

A WORLD OF IDEAS:
SEE ALL THERE IS TO KNOW

www.dk.com

Contents

Two-toed sloths and three-toed sloths

There are two families of sloth. You can spot the difference by counting the toes on their front legs.

Three-toed sloths are smaller than two-toed sloths. They have dark marks around their eyes. Their front legs are longer than their back legs.

Three-toed sloths have a longer neck.

Three toes with claws

Three-toed sloths have a tail.

Two-toed sloths move more between trees.

Two toes with claws

Two-toed sloths have bigger noses than three-toed sloths. They are also larger and move more quickly.

Two-toed sloths have larger eyes.

5

Chapter 1
Let's meet
the sloths

Shhhhh! This little baby is asleep. It hangs on to its mother's fur as it snoozes. Mom is sound asleep, too. These drowsy mammals are sloths.

Sloths live high up in the trees in Central and South America. They hardly ever come down! There are plenty of leaves, buds, and shoots for these vegetarians to eat.

Sloths move very slowly. This makes it hard for other animals to spot them in the trees.

Sloths hide by living high in the trees. They hang for hours using their long arms. Sloths' organs are attached to their bones. This means the organs won't squash their lungs when sloths dangle upside down from trees.

Long, curved claws help sloths to hang from trees.

Sloth species

There are six species of sloth that hang from the trees. Let's meet them!

Linnaeus's two-toed sloth: This sloth is about the size of a small dog.

Maned three-toed sloth: With black hairs on its neck and shoulders, this rare sloth lives in Brazil.

Pale-throated three-toed sloth: This sloth has poor eyesight and hearing.

Pygmy three-toed sloth: This is the smallest sloth and is an excellent swimmer.

Hoffman's two-toed sloth: With extra-long claws, these sloths can climb high.

Brown-throated three-toed sloth: A curved mouth makes this sloth look like it is always smiling.

Chapter 2
Growing up

Squeak! A baby sloth talks to its mom. It holds on to her front, not her back like other animals. Mom and baby stay together for a whole year or more. The little one licks some food scraps from around the mom's mouth. Soon, it will munch its own meals.

Moms and babies stay together, but most adult sloths live alone.

The mother sloth shows her baby how to climb through the treetops. Claws and strong muscles give sloths a good grip.

Mostly, the baby gives its mom an all-day hug. Oops! Sometimes the little sloth slips off. However, it climbs back up again.

Once a week, sloths leave
their treetop homes. They climb
down to the forest floor to poop.
The sloths crawl around.
Their long claws make
walking tricky. Their
back legs are not
very strong.

Splash! Sloths drop right into the water from the trees. Their long arms make them good swimmers.

They speed through the water more quickly than they move on land. After a swim, it's time for more sleeping.

The sloth swims using a stroke similar to the doggy paddle.

Where do sloths live?

The tall trees in forests are home to sloths. Sloths live on the continents of Central and South America.

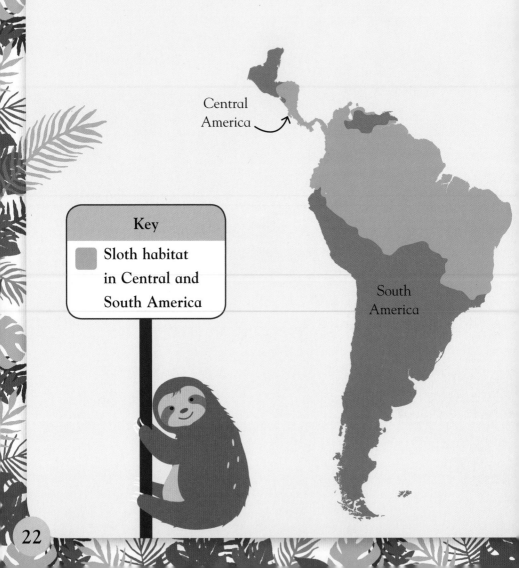

Central America

South America

Key

Sloth habitat in Central and South America

Forest habitats

Deciduous forests:
Trees lose their leaves in this kind of forest. It is home to Hoffman's two-toed sloths.

Tropical forests:
The trees in tropical forests have thick branches, which help sloths to hide.

Red Mangrove forests:
The pygmy three-toed sloth is found in the red mangrove trees.

Rain forests:
Rain forests give shelter to plenty of sloths from two- and three-toed families.

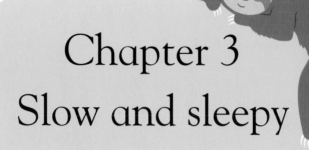

Chapter 3
Slow and sleepy

Don't ask a sloth to slow down. They are the slowest-moving mammals around! Up in the trees, they rarely move faster than 7 ft (215 cm) per minute. On the ground, they are even slower. They crawl about 1 ft (30 cm) a minute. They do this to save energy.

Sloths hardly ever come down to the ground.

Sleeping so much helps sloths save energy, too. Sloths are among the biggest snoozers in the animal kingdom. Wild sloths nap for around 10 hours a day. In zoos, they sleep for as much as 15 hours.

Sloths can sleep even while hanging upside down.

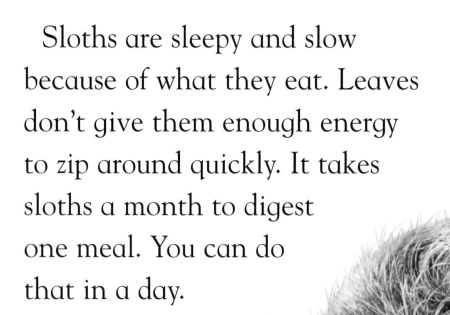

Sloths are sleepy and slow because of what they eat. Leaves don't give them enough energy to zip around quickly. It takes sloths a month to digest one meal. You can do that in a day.

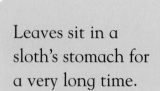

Leaves sit in a sloth's stomach for a very long time.

Chapter 4
Sloth survival

Sloths must be extra careful when they visit the forest floor. Jaguars and pumas are on the prowl.

Sloths cannot run away from danger. They do have other ways to protect themselves, though.

Jaguar

Puma

Staying up high in the trees helps sloths to hide. They don't make sudden movements. Sloths can also turn their heads nearly all the way around. This means they can spot something sneaking up behind them.

Hanging so high up makes it hard for other animals to see or get to sloths.

Sloth fur also helps them stay hidden. Tiny, plant-like algae grows on sloth fur.

The algae makes their fur look green! It sounds weird, but it helps them blend in with the leaves.

If a sloth does get into a tricky situation, it uses its claws to defend itself. It swipes its claws at the predator to hurt or scare it away. Then it scrambles back to safety in the branches.

A three-toed sloth showing its claws.

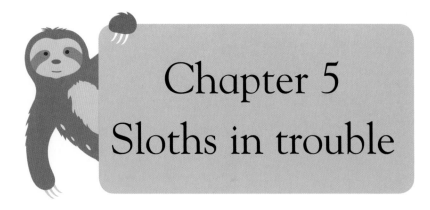

Chapter 5
Sloths in trouble

There's something that stops sloths from smiling. That's us. People love to hold sloths and take photos with them. These sloths are often taken from the wild. If they are not cared for properly, they can die.

Sloths are at risk in other ways, too. People are cutting down the trees where sloths live. Tourists can damage habitats. This had led to the pygmy sloth nearly dying out.

Some sloth habitats have been destroyed.

There are still people looking out for sloths. They want to protect them. Hopefully more sloths can sleep safely. Sweet dreams!

Baby sloths at the Sloth Sanctuary
in Costa Rica.

Fun facts about sloths

Sloths may be sleepy, but there are plenty of eye-opening facts to learn about them.

Sloths are three times faster in water than they are on land.

Giant ground sloths lived 10,000 years ago. The extinct Megatherium was the largest.

Sloths give birth while hanging upside down.

The world's only sloth orphanage is in Costa Rica, Central America.

Sloths don't sweat and have no body odor.

Quiz

 1. How many hours a day can a sloth sleep?

 2. In what parts of the world do sloths live?

 3. Why do sloths leave the treetops?

 4. What do sloths mainly eat?

 5. Sloths are slow movers. Do you know why?

 6. Why do some sloths have green fur?

7 What are the names of the two families of sloths?

8 What is the smallest sloth?

9 Name two animals that hunt sloths.

10 Where do sloths move faster, on land or in water?

Answers to the quiz:

1. 10–15 hours a day; 2. Central and South America; 3. To poop; 4. Leaves, buds, and shoots; 5. Because of their leafy diet, and to avoid being hunted; 6. Tiny, plant-like algae grows on them; 7. Two-toed and three-toed sloths; 8. Pygmy three-toed sloth; 9. Jaguars and pumas; 10. In water

Glossary

algae
simple plant that grows in sloth fur. Seaweed is a type of algae

claw
name for a curved nail on the toes of a bird, lizard, or mammal

drowsy
very sleepy and tired

habitat
home or environment where an animal lives

mammal
warm-blooded animal that has fur, and makes milk to feed its young

predator
animal that hunts other animals for food

rain forest
lush, dense forest found in tropical areas, with heavy rainfall

species
type of animal or plant with shared features that can produce young together

vegetarian
animal that does not eat meat

Index

A LEVEL FOR EVERY READER

This book is a part of an exciting four-level reading series to support children in developing the habit of reading widely for both pleasure and information. Each book is designed to develop a child's reading skills, fluency, grammar awareness, and comprehension in order to build confidence and enjoyment when reading.

Ready for a Level 2 (Beginning to Read) book

A child should:

- be able to recognize a bank of common words quickly and be able to blend sounds together to make some words.
- be familiar with using beginner letter sounds and context clues to figure out unfamiliar words.
- sometimes correct his/her reading if it doesn't look right or make sense.
- be aware of the need for a slight pause at commas and a longer one at periods.

A valuable and shared reading experience

For many children, reading requires much effort, but adult participation can make reading both fun and easier. Here are a few tips on how to use this book with a young reader:

Check out the contents together:

- read about the book on the back cover and talk about the contents page to help heighten interest and expectation.
- discuss new or difficult words.
- chat about labels, annotations, and pictures.

Support the reader:

- give the book to the young reader to turn the pages.
- where necessary, encourage longer words to be broken into syllables, sound out each one, and then flow the syllables together; ask him/her to reread the sentence to check the meaning.
- encourage the reader to vary her/his voice as she/he reads; demonstrate how to do this if helpful.

Talk at the end of each book, or after every few pages:

- ask questions about the text and the meaning of the words used—this helps develop comprehension skills.
- read the quiz at the end of the book and encourage the reader to answer the questions, if necessary, by turning back to the relevant pages to find the answers.

Series consultant, Dr. Linda Gambrell, Distinguished Professor of Education at Clemson University, has served as President of the National Reading Conference, the College Reading Association, and the International Reading Association.